HAY FEVER

by

Aug Hoppin

A.W.W

PUBLISHED BY J.R. OSGOOD & Co.
BOSTON. 1873.

The "Hay Fever."

*"The **Autumnal** Catarrh commences the last week in August, **and** continues till the last week in September. It begins with sneezing, itching of the eyes (especially at the inner corners), watering of the eyes, &c., &c. . . . The affection of the eyes is in fits, coming on suddenly, compelling the sufferer to rub his eyes violently for relief. The fits of sneezing and nose-blowing and obstruction of the nostrils, are also sudden. . . . The disease subsides during the third week in September. . . . Fortunately the study of the natural history of the disease has shown us a remedy which is successful in all its periods.*

"A removal to a non-catarrhal region.—This is the great, not to say the only remedy. . . . Among the most prominent and general causes of paroxysms is the dust and smoke of a railroad train, sunshine, fruits of various kinds, the fragrance of flowers, &c., &c." — Extract from Dr. Wyman's book on Autumnal Catarrh.

Dr. Oliver Wendell Holmes in reply to Rev. Henry Ward Beecher as to a remedy for Hay Fever :—

"Gravel is an effectual cure. It should be taken about eight feet deep."

"I have a salt and sullen rheum offends me.
Lend me thy handkerchief." — Othello, Act iii., Scene iv.

"Tears, idle tears." — Tennyson.

I. At midnight, on the 19th of August, Mr. A. Wiper Weeps is awakened with an irritation of the eyes, and remarks to Mrs. Weeps that he "feels it coming on."

II. Whereupon he jumps out of bed, and grinds his eyes with both his fists.

III. Becoming weary, he implores his partner to help him.

IV. She wakes the children to aid her.

V. He tries to scratch the roof of his mouth with the back of his tongue: his wife and children think he is "mad."

VI. Discouraged condition of Mr. Weeps after four days of "sneezing and weeping."

VII. 1. He tries Allopathy by the bucketful. 2. He takes Homœopathy through a magnifying-glass. 3. He indulges in a pinch of the "Great Anti-Catarrh Snuff," which completely upsets him.

VIII. Hearing that the seaside is a specific for the "Hay-fever," he takes a fresh handkerchief, and hurries to the station.

IX. The railway dust "sets him wild:" so Mr. Weeps arranges himself for the journey, and becomes an object of curiosity to his fellow-travellers.

X. Mr. Weeps's first week's wash by the seashore.

XI. He tries sea-bathing, but, caught between a sneeze and a breaker, is hurried to land the wrong way.

XII. *It seemed as if Mr. Weeps never would stop sneezing, when a young lady from Philadelphia innocently insisted upon presenting him with a bunch of the "Rosa rubiginosa" ("Rub in your nose, sir"), which grew so plentifully in that vicinity.*

XIII. At night, Mr. Weeps (propped up with pillows) gradually sinks into an uneasy slumber; but his frantic efforts to catch his breath startle the boarders, who think "it's burglars."

XIV. In despair, Mr. Weeps retreats from the seaside to the dryer atmosphere of the country

XV. Mr. Weeps among the hills. His second week's wash at an elevation of one mile

XVI. His continuous "snuffing and blowing" so disturb the country "meetin'," that the elders eject Mr. Weeps as a nuisance.

XVII. His existence in the country being no longer agreeable, he seeks the bowels of the earth, and tries a coal-mine.

XVIII. The coal-dust "sets him frantic:" so he flies to the Indian country, and becomes a companion of the Prairie-Dog: but that affords him no relief.

XIX. Hearing there is a cure beyond the "non-catarrhal region," he clutches his handkerchief-box, and clambers the Rocky Mountains in search of it.

XX. Exhausted, Mr. Weeps falls asleep on top of the Sierras, while his handkerchiefs are drying in the morning sun.

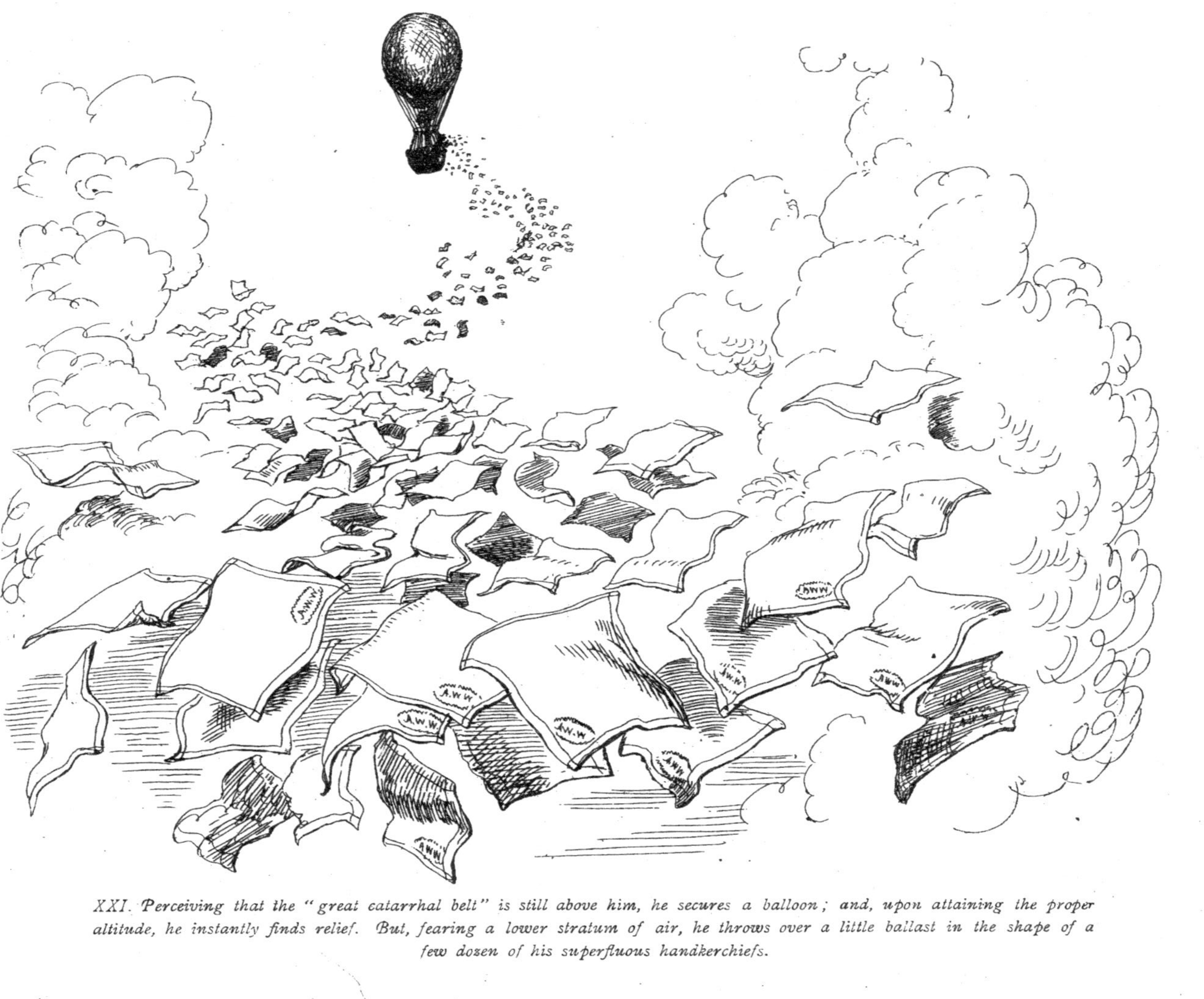

XXI. Perceiving that the "great catarrhal belt" is still above him, he secures a balloon; and, upon attaining the proper altitude, he instantly finds relief. But, fearing a lower stratum of air, he throws over a little ballast in the shape of a few dozen of his superfluous handkerchiefs.

XXII. Mr. Weeps, after floating about for a week in space, chooses a sunny day for his fifth-weeks' wash.

XXIII. On the 25th of September Mr. Weeps "pulls the valve," and alights upon the earth again, somewhat thinner in flesh, but entirely cured of his disease.

XXIV. Mrs. Weeps putting away her husband's handkerchiefs in readiness for the next "annual attack."

www.ingramcontent.com/pod-product-compliance
Lightning Source LLC
LaVergne TN
LVHW020742120826
845150LV00010B/2354

* 9 7 8 1 4 1 8 1 9 3 7 2 0 *